To Ida
+ Frank
from Tom & List

Christmas
1992

FAMILY · TIES

Edited by
Beth Mende Conny

Designed by
SCHARR DESIGN

PETER **P**AUPER **P**RESS, **I**NC.
WHITE PLAINS · NEW YORK

For my husband Joe and daughter Julia

Table of Contents

Family Ties
Quotations About the Family

When we hold hands, my fingers smile.
Beth Mende Conny,
about her family

Introduction

"Other things may change us," Anthony Brandt once wrote, "but we all start and end with the family."

We're all born into a family, after all, and within that powerful, emotionally charged unit, we become more than just ourselves; we become sons, daughters, sisters, brothers, mothers, fathers, grandmothers and grand-fathers. The roles we play, and the relationships we enter by virtue of our birth, clearly shape, color and enrich our lives. We are each unique because of our shared experience of family.

Family Ties is a celebration of that shared experience. It's also an exploration of contemporary family life. For families, like the times, have changed. They've taken on new challenges and new compositions. No longer does the "traditional" family represent the majority of American families. Today, the "nontraditional" family—with its step-parents, single parents and working moms— is in fact the norm.

The quotations selected for this collection reflect these changes. They also touch upon the experiences that have always been a part of family life, be they the joy of a child's birth or the sadness of a parent's death, the love between parent and child or the hostility between siblings, the challenge of living within a tight family budget, or the trauma of living with a rebellious teen.

The quotations themselves have been culled from the works of well-known writers, child care experts, politicians, philosophers, scientists, humorists, and pundits. Taken together, they offer pearls of wit, wisdom and warmth, entertainment and comfort. They also serve as a reminder of just how special and important families are to lives. For as Sam Levenson said, families are our "first and most influential school." They are the places in which we create our future.

B.M.C.

The Family Album

Other things may change us, but we all start and end with the family.

Anthony Brandt

The family you come from isn't as important as the family you're going to have.

Ring Lardner

The immediate family consists of whomever you would expect to rally around you if you were suddenly poor and undeserving.

Judith Martin (Miss Manners)

All happy families are alike, but each unhappy family is unhappy in its own way.

Leo Tolstoy

Politeness, that cementer of friendship and soother of enmities, is nowhere so much required, and so frequently outraged, as in family circles.

Marguerite Blessington

Raising a family is a meditation.

Joseph Campbell

No matter how many communes anybody invents, the family always creeps back.

Margaret Mead

What it really means to be a parent—note this carefully, because it's the essence of the whole thing—is: You will spend an enormous portion of your time lurking outside public-toilet stalls.

Dave Barry

Rejoice with your family in the beautiful
land of life.

Albert Einstein

Parents become, effortlessly, just by showing
up, the most influential totems in the lives of
their children.

Anna Quindlen

Giving birth is an experience and parenthood
is a state of being; the one passes, the other
never ends.

Joyce Maynard

God deserts those who break away from
their families.

Spanish Proverb

Child raising is a crash course in self-knowledge.

Ellen Goodman

Raising children is a creative endeavor, an art rather than a science.

Bruno Bettelheim

The principal goal of parenting is teaching children to become their own parents.

Wayne W. Dyer

Your responsibility as a parent is not as great as you might imagine. You need not supply the world with the next conqueror of disease or major motion-picture star. If your child simply grows up to be someone who does not use the word "collectible" as a noun, you can consider yourself an unqualified success.

Fran Lebowitz

Sad to say, the strain of being a parent unhinges many minds, and opens those minds to the unsound ideas of advanced thinkers.

George F. Will

Is it not strange that he who has no children beings them up so well?

Confucius

In our age of professionalism, many people have lost sight of the *real* child-rearing experts—parents themselves.

Jo Ann Miller and Susan Weissman

A mother is someone who: looks forward to getting a root canal so she can sit quietly in one place; thinks a meaningful conversation with her husband is an uninterrupted sentence; worries her kid won't have a prom date even though he's still in daycare; and would have kids all over again, despite what she knows.

Beth Mende Conny

Mothers are people who fold over your
peanut-butter sandwiches for you.

Robert Paul Smith

A lover loves one day, a mother all her life.

Spanish Proverb

To be a really good, creative mother you
have to be an extraordinary woman. You
have to keep yourself involved with your
child during great periods of the day when
it's just the two of you and you feel that at
any moment you may literally go out of your
mind.

Meryl Streep

There's only one pretty child in the world,
and every mother has it.

J. C. Bridge

Children are the anchors that hold a mother to life.

Sophocles

In my mom's closet there were always two dresses. They were clean, they were in great shape, but there were only two. My parents were people who never had anything, but they had everything.

Mike Krzyzewski

One often wonders where mothers learn all about the things they tell their daughters not to do.

Unknown

Clever father, clever daughter; clever mother, clever son.

Russian Proverb

There was a time when Mrs. Einstein knew a lot more than Albert.

Marguerite Kelly

You have to dig deep to bury your Daddy.

Gypsy Proverb

When I was a boy, no boy ever said he wanted to grow up and be a father. Hopefully, that is changing.

John Byrne Barry

It is a wise father that knows his own child.

William Shakespeare

Be a father to your children. If they want an entertainer, let them hire one.

Sam Levenson

What you have inherited from your father you must earn over again for yourselves or it will not be yours.

Goethe

A man can be loved by millions, but that has to be no consolation at all if he can't bring his own love to his child.

Bob Greene

Only when you become a father will you learn how to be a son.

Spanish Proverb

There must always be a struggle between a father and son, while one aims at power and the other at independence.

Samuel Johnson

Father and son are natural enemies and each is happier and more secure in keeping it that way.

John Steinbeck

The worst misfortune that can happen to an ordinary man is to have an extraordinary father.

Austin O'Malley

A child is the only known substance from which a responsible adult can be made.

Thomas Lickona

The trouble with children is that they are not returnable.

Quentin Crisp

I love children, especially when they cry, for then someone takes them away.

Nancy Mitford

You can't trust kids; they'll grow up while your back is turned.

Teresa Bloomingdale

Children have neither past nor future; they enjoy the present, which very few of us do.

La Bruyère

The childhood shows the man,
As morning shows the day.

John Milton

Childhood is the most basic human right of
children.

David Elkind

There is always one moment in childhood
when the door opens and lets in the future.

Graham Greene

True sibling relationships have a varied lot of
ingredients, but sympathy is rarely one of
them.

Judith Martin (Miss Manners)

Children. You can't live with them and you can't live with them.

Robin Williams

No two children are ever born into the exact same family.

Seymour V. Reit

Grandparents are people who play with children whether they are busy or not.

Lanie Carter

He who after raising his own children raises also his grandchildren is a big fool.

Spanish Proverb

We have yet to meet a kid stupid enough to show pictures of his grandparents to total strangers on a bus, let alone repeat the clever things they say.

Compiled by Sam Levenson

Why do grandparents and grandchildren get along so well? They have the same enemy: the parents.

Anonymous

One of life's greatest mysteries is how the boy who wasn't good enough to marry your daughter can be the father of the smartest grandchild in the world.

Jewish Proverb

Family tree: the only tree whose branches seek the shelter of its roots.

Unknown

My recommendation to any kid planning to have a nice permissive childhood is to have loving parents who come to see him often, treat him with generosity and affection, and leave him in the care of an infatuated grandmother.

Ed McMahon

A person who always brags about his ancestors is like a potato—the best part of him is underground.

Yiddish Proverb

Blood is thicker than water—and it boils quicker.

Unknown

Don't try to marry an entire family or it may work out that way.

George Ade

Family Timelines

If pregnancy were a book they would cut the last two chapters.

Nora Ephron

I think most people should be discouraged from having children, because most people have no gift for parenthood. Most parents realize this eventually. The children, of course, realize it right away.

Gore Vidal

Families with babies and families without babies are sorry for each other.

Edgar Watson Howe

Wondering if having kids will change your life is like wondering if nuclear winter will affect the way you tan.

Beth Mende Conny

I find that the most successful approach to the subject of babies is to discuss them as though they were hams; the firmness of the flesh, the pinkness of the flesh, the even distribution of fat, the sweetness and tenderness of the whole, and the placing of bone are the things to praise.

Samuel Marchbanks

Maternity is a matter of fact; paternity always a matter of opinion.

Unknown

The one unifying, incontrovertible experience shared by all women and men is that months-long period we spent unfolding inside a woman's body.

Adrienne Rich

There comes a point in a pregnancy . . . when the body and the mind get pretty much overtaken, and every inch is occupied territory.

Joyce Maynard

I love this little life! With all the pain of it, I long for the wonderful thing to happen, for a tiny human creature to spring from between my limbs bravely out into the world. I need it, just as a poet *needs* to create an undying work.

Yang Ping

The first cry of a newborn baby in Chicago or Zamboango, in Amsterdam or Rangoon, has the same pitch and key, each saying, "I am! I have come through! I belong! I am a member of the Family!"

Carl Sandburg

A man and a woman have a child; for a period of time it is as if they are the only three people in the world.

Bob Greene

It takes three to make a birthday.

Penelope Leach

To my embarrassment I was born in bed with a lady.

Wilson Mizner

Begetting children is a delightful duty.

Plautus

My obstetrician was so dumb that when I gave birth he forgot to cut the cord. For a year that kid followed me *everywhere*. It was like having a dog on a leash.

Joan Rivers

The night you were born, I ceased being my father's boy and became my son's father. That night I began a new life.

Henry Gregor Felsen

I knew the baby was going to change my life, but I didn't expect her to define it.

Bob Greene

There are actually two transitions to parenthood: his and hers.

Carolyn Paper Cowen

The first baby is born to a couple, whereas the second baby is born to a family.

Seymour V. Reit

A baby is an angel whose wings get smaller as its legs get taller.

Anonymous

Babies control and bring up their families as much as they are controlled by them; in fact, we may say that the family brings up a baby by being brought up by him.

Erik Erikson

My mother didn't breast-feed me. She said she liked me as a friend.

Rodney Dangerfield

A new baby is like the beginning of all things—wonder, hope, a dream of possibilities.

Eda J. Leshan

When we can hear the baby laugh, it is the loveliest thing that can happen to us.

Sigmund Freud

Those boyhood memories! I have them
often, although I can control them pretty
well with medication!

Dave Barry

When I was younger I could remember
anything whether it happened or not.

Mark Twain

The young have no depth perception in
time. Ten years back or 10 years forward is
an eternity.

Robert C. Alberts

I have been slow to understand that the
contrariness of the "terrible twos" is the
bloody-mindedness of little people trying to
get a grip on their partially formed selves.

George F. Will

In youth time flies upon a silken wing.

Katharine Augusta Ware

The real menace in dealing with a five-year-old is that in no time at all you begin to sound like a five-year-old.

Jean Kerr

An interesting personality is, in an adult, insufferable. In a teenager it is frequently punishable by law.

Fran Lebowitz

If there's one thing tougher than being a teenager, it's having one.

Gordon McLean

Adolescence: that period when children feel
their parents should be told the facts of life.

Unknown

During adolescence, your boy has the soul of
a poet and the carnal appetites of a tomcat,
so it's no wonder his judgments are as
erratic as his emotions.

Joseph H. Peck

Adolescence is the age when a girl's voice
changes from no to yes.

Anonymous

Up to sixteen, a lad is a Boy Scout. After that
he is a girl scout.

Unknown

We spend half our lives unlearning the follies transmitted to us by our parents, and the other half transmitting our own follies to our offspring.

Isaac Goldbert

Moving an inch with your parents is like progressing a mile with the rest of the world.

Elizabeth Carter

What do you do with mother love and mother wit when the babies are grown and gone away?

Joanne Greenberg

When a woman is twenty, a child deforms her; when she is thirty, he preserves her; and when forty, he makes her young again.

Léon Blum

If the daughter marry well, thou hast found a son; if not, thou hast lost a daughter.

Quarles

No matter how old a mother is, she watches her middle-aged children for signs of improvement.

Florida Scott-Maxwell

The best revenge is to live long enough to be a problem to your children.

Unknown

If you believe your parents' problems are not yours but strictly theirs, you would have to agree that a stick has one end.

James Halpern

Inner Landscapes

Give a child an inch and he'll think he's a
ruler.

Compiled by Sam Levenson

All the world loves a winner, but a child
needs to know his parents love him when he
wins, when he loses and when he just chugs
along.

Marguerite Kelly

Allow children to be happy their own way;
for what better way will they ever find?

Samuel Johnson

We set the stage for the young persons, but
they are the playwrights.

Helene Arnstein

Nothing has a stronger influence psychologically on their environment, and especially on their children, than the unlived life of the parents.

Carl Jung

When a child is given the power to activate our guilt, it is like handing him an atomic bomb.

Haim G. Ginott

When your child has a difficult time, it's only natural to blame yourself and think, "What did I do wrong?" But some children are just born a certain way, and there's very little you can do about it.

Nancy Reagan

You would miss the guilt trips if your folks weren't around to send you on them.

Lewis Grizzard

If you listen, you might hear. If you hear, you might mix up what they say with what you fear or imagine. It's a lot smarter or safer, if you want the news, to buy the *Enquirer.*

Delia Ephron

Children have never been very good at listening to their elders, but they have never failed to imitate them.

James Baldwin

Teach your child to hold his tongue; he'll learn fast enough to speak.

Benjamin Franklin

Parents are usually unaware that their reasons and behavior make as little sense to their child as his do to them.

Bruno Bettelheim

I don't believe in majority rule in the family—especially if you have three kids.

Ed Bliss

Sometimes I think I'll never understand children, and the only solution is for them to grow up so they can understand me.

Jack Paar

No matter how much kids seem to resent authority, they resent even more being left with none at all.

Art Linkletter

Our dilemma as parents: how to give our child what she wants and still not feel like total suckers.

Alice Kahn

The path to the self-disciplined child is the path forged by the self-disciplined adult.

Peter Ernest Haiman

Obstinacy in children is like a kite; it is kept up just as long as we pull against it.

Marcelene Cox

Let your children be more in awe of your kindness than of your power.

Savile

Children. Surely if those kids knew they needed love, they'd be more lovable.

Jean Kerr

Kids get in trouble, but it's human nature to get as close to the hot stove as you can — and sometimes you touch it.

John Wayne

Children . . . are the last candid audience left. They don't care what critics say and they will let you know immediately what delights and what bores them.

Gian-Carlo Menotti

What a distressing contrast there is between the radiant intelligence of the child and the feeble mentality of the average adult.

Sigmund Freud

There is no fear as great and as deeply instinctive in a small child as that of being left alone.

T. Berry Brazelton

The playing adult steps sideward into
another reality; the playing child advances
forward to new stages of mastery.

Erik Erikson

Children use fantasy not to get out of, but to
get into, the real world.

John Holt

The child sees everything which has to be
experienced and learned as a doorway. So
does the adult. But what to the child is an
entrance is to the adult only a passage.

Friedrich Nietzsche

If, in instructing a child, you are vexed with
it for want of adroitness, try, if you have
never tried before, to write with your left
hand, and then remember that a child is all
left hand.

J. F. Boyse

Scenes of Everyday Life

What seems to be the most needed in the modern home is the family.

Unknown

Home is the place where, when you have to go there, they have to take you in.

Robert Frost

Home is the place where we create the future.

T. Berry Brazelton

A child is fed with milk and praise.

Mary Anne Lamb

Imagine the whole family—parent, lover, friend, toddler, and teenager—in the same room at the same time without the distractions of play or work. Imagine them focused on one another, sharing experiences, solving problems, asking questions, watching reactions, teaching, learning, listening. In most households, those seemingly utopian encounters already happen, or could, every evening—and they're called dinnertimes.

Letty Cottin Pogrebin

Children never want to eat in restaurants. What they want to do is play under the table until the entrees arrive, then go to the bathroom.

Dave Barry

This would be a better world for children if parents had to eat the spinach.

Groucho Marx

Girls like to dress up. Boys like to dress down.

Stanton Delaplane

It now costs more to amuse a child than it did to educate his father.

Anonymous

One father can support ten children, but ten children seem unable to support one father.

Jewish Saying

Only a mother can understand how a budget that cannot tolerate a winter coat for herself can come up with enough cash to send her high school senior on a ski trip.

Teresa Bloomingdale

There is in every child at every stage a new miracle of vigorous unfolding, which constitutes a new hope and a new responsibility for all.

Erik Erikson

Do not join encounter groups. If you enjoy being made to feel inadequate, call your mother.

Liz Smith

Prolonged adolescence was invented in the 20th century so that there would be somebody to use the telephone in the afternoon. . . . Before the telephone, there were no teenagers.

John Leonard

A pedestrian is a man whose son is home from college.

Unknown

Hardly any homes have any intellectual life whatsoever, let alone one that informs the vital interests of life. Educational TV marks the high tide for family intellectual life.

Allan Bloom

TV: The Third Parent

R. Buckminster Fuller

Everywhere I go, kids walk around not with books under their arms, but with radios up against their heads. Children can't read or write, but they can memorize whole albums.

Rev. Jesse Jackson

A mere parent pitted against a child in a test of wills in a toy store is a terrible spectacle.

George F. Will

The pupil who is never required to do what he cannot do, never does what he can do.

John Stuart Mill

All our schools are finishing schools; they finish what has never been begun.

G. K. Chesterton

A child educated only at school is an uneducated child.

George Santayana

Smartness runs in my family. When I went to school I was so smart my teacher was in my class for five years.

George Burns

When you are dissatisfied and would like to go back to your youth, think of Algebra.

Gene Yasenak

One bad report card does not mean the end of the world. (Two, on the other hand, just might.)

Teresa Bloomingdale

An *F* on an exam is a failed exam, not a failed child.

Penny Coleman

Be cool, stay in school. That's where the sex and drugs are.

Anonymous

College: A bar with a $15,000 cover charge.

Anonymous

You can lead a boy to college but you cannot make him think.

Elbert Hubbard

The use of a university is to make young gentlemen as unlike their fathers as possible.

Woodrow Wilson

Don't bother discussing sex with small children. They rarely have anything to add.

Fran Lebowitz

Sex is a three-letter word which sometimes needs some old-fashioned four-letter words to convey its full meaning: words like *help, give, care, kiss, feel, love,* words which even a child can understand.

Sam Levenson

Sex drive: A physical craving that begins in adolescence and ends at marriage.

Robert Byrne

Often a girl plays at sex, for which she's not ready, because what she wants is love; and a boy plays at love, for which he's not ready, because what he wants is sex.

Gordon McLean

Many a girl has gotten into trouble by obeying that boyological urge.

Katharine Brush

Some of our modern children are so precocious, the birds and the bees should study them.

Chester L. Marks

My schoolmates would make love to anything that moved, but I never saw any reason to limit myself.

Emo Philips

Like most hurts the young endure, a lack of popularity is easier for a girl to bear if her mother is not crushed by it.

Edith Neisser

If God wanted sex to be fun, He wouldn't have included children as punishment.

Ed Bluestone

Toddlers are famous for wandering around at the strangest times and, of course, the first place they make for is Mother's bedroom.

William Reynolds

She never quite leaves her children at home, even when she doesn't take them along.

Margaret Culkin Banning

There are two classes of travel—first class, and with children.

Robert Benchley

This year we've decided to send the dogs to camp and the kids to obedience school.

Anonymous

Summer camps—those places where little boys go for mother's vacation.

Unknown

Changing Times/
Changing Families

Your basic extended family today includes
your ex-husband or -wife, your ex's new
mate, your new mate, possibly your new
mate's ex, and any new mate that your new
mate's ex has acquired. It consists entirely of
people who are not related by blood, many
of whom can't stand each other.

Delia Ephron

Sacred family! . . . The supposed home of all
the virtues, where innocent children are
tortured into their first falsehoods, where
wills are broken by parental tyranny, and
self-respect is smothered by crowded,
jostling egos.

August Strindberg

Parents may get divorced, but they never
divorce their children.

Anonymous

When I can no longer bear to think of the victims of broken homes, I begin to think of the victims of intact ones.

Peter de Vries

To children, the voluntary separation of parents seems worse than their death precisely because it is voluntary.

Allan Bloom

We would have broken up except for the children. Who were the children? Well, she and I were.

Mort Sahl

If you choose to continue your warfare with your child's mother, you can turn your child into a war orphan.

Gerald Hill

Just as instant love is a fantasy ideal in stepfamilies, so, too, is the concept of instant parent.

Seymour V. Reit

Almost every little girl grows up hoping to be a mother someday. But has there ever been one who dreamed of becoming a stepmother?

Evelyn Bassoff

Stepmothers have always had bad press.

Emily Visher

In our clockwork world, it can take practice for adults to change over every so often to Children's Standard Time.

Fred Rogers and Barry Head

The best inheritance a parent can give his children is a few minutes of his time each day.

O. A. Battista

By worrying about the past and future, we lose the present and our children don't have us, even when we are around.

David Elkind

The fear that the child will not gain a place on the overcrowded fast track can turn babyhood into a chronic dash for achievement.

Andree Aelion Brooks

Children feel they have all the time in the world; to encourage their worldly explorations, we need to cultivate the same feelings in ourselves.

Diane McClain Bengson

Every mother is a working mother and many of them get paid for it.

Marguerite Kelly

Working mothers often feel poised between the cultures of the housewife and the working man.

Arlie Hochschild

In many ways, today's Superwoman is Everywoman.

Marjorie Hansen Shaevitz

Blessed are the young, for they shall inherit the national debt.

Herbert Hoover

One hesitates to bring a child into this world without fixing it up a little.

Alta

If I had influence with the good fairy who is supposed to preside over the christening of all children I should ask that her gift to each child in the world be a sense of wonder so indestructible that it would last throughout life, as an unfailing antidote against the boredom and disenchantments of later years, the sterile preoccupation with things that are artificial, the alienation from the sources of strength.

Rachel Carson

In a secular age, children have become the last sacred objects.

Joseph Epstein

The future of the world would be assured if every child were loved.

Bernie Siegel